PORTLAND'S PUBLIC ART

A Guide and History

Norma Catherine Gleason

Chet Orloff

Western Imprints
The Press of the Oregon Historical Society
&
Metropolitan Arts Commission

The Metropolitan Arts Commission, a joint agency of the city of Portland and Multnomah County, works to support the arts and to enrich the cultural life of the metropolitan area. The Commission provides direct grants to artists and arts organizations through its Grants-in Service program; administers the One Percent for Public Art Program; publishes a newsletter; offers workshops and other forms of technical assistance; represents the arts in public forums; and serves as an informational resource to citizens of the area.

Cover: Profile of *Portlandia*, from a preliminary study by the sculptor Raymond Kaskey.
Frontis: *Skidmore Fountain* by Olin L. Warner, M48 (OHS Neg. 69076). Photo by John Bauguess.

Library of Congress Cataloging in Publication Data

Gleason, Norma Catherine, 1951-
  Portland's public art.

  Includes index.
  1. Urban beautification—Oregon—Portland. 2. Art, Municipal—Oregon—Portland. 3. Portland (Ore.)—Public works. I. Orloff, Chet, 1949- II. Title.
NA9052.G43 1983 917.95'49 83-10460
ISBN 0-87595-059-0 (pbk.)

Printed in the United States of America.

This volume was designed and produced by Western Imprints, the Press of the Oregon Historical Society.

DEDICATION

To Frances J. Murname (longshoreman and life-long preservationist) and all others who have supported and preserved Portland's public art.

CONTENTS

ACKNOWLEDGMENTS

In grateful appreciation of their generous donations of time, information and energy, we would like to thank:

John Bauguess for his photographs
Herbert K. Beals for his maps
Liisa Fagerlund and Stan Parr of the city of Portland
  Records Office
Polly Eyerly and Evelyn Lamon of the Portland Art
  Association
The Portland Landmarks Commission
Jack Eyerly
Arthur Spencer and Evelyn Hicks
  of the Oregon Historical Society
Michele Russo
Wendy Wells of the Fountain Gallery of Art
Father Gabriel Webber of the Grotto
Ruth B. Selid of the Portland Bureau of Parks and
  Public Recreation
Warren Iliff and Susan Ford of the Washington Park
  Zoo
Hilda Morris
Tom Hardy
Frederick Heidel
Michihuro Kosuge
Peter Flahoss of Lewis and Clark College
Katherine Corbett of Portland State University
Dr. Mary Margaret Dundore of the University of
  Portland
Julie Reiss and Charles Rhyne of Reed College
May Fadaak

Catlin Gabel School
William Alfstad of the Oregon School of Arts and Crafts
Emily Carpenter
Marianne Littman
Nancy Lindburg of the Oregon Arts Commission
Temple Beth Israel
The *Oregonian* Library
The Arlington Club
Christopher Kopca of the Portland Development Commission
Paul J. Alexander of the Federal General Services Administration
Lorenzo Ghiglieri
Rachael Griffin
Stuart Durkheimer
Einas Flodin
Steve Cuckley
Elizabeth Leach of the Leach Gallery of Art
Sister Joan Hansen of St. Mary's Academy
Margo Jacobsen of the Lawrence Gallery
Janet Stevens of St. Francis Assisi Park
The Japanese Garden Society

Publication of the Guide was made possible in part by a grant from the Oregon Committee for the Humanities through a grant from the National Endowment for the Humanities, a federal agency established by an act of Congress in 1965.

x

INTRODUCTION

Writing a guide to Portland's public art is a little like writing one's family history: the ink is hardly dry before another baby is born and an unhappy cousin calls to say that his branch of the family tree was omitted. We emphasize that this small book is not an all-inclusive catalogue, but a guide to over 200 Portland works of public art which we believe are permanently sited and easily accessible to pedestrians.

Portland's public art has benefited from a century of generous private and public patronage. Since the 1970s, when the state of Oregon instituted one percent for public art for new buildings and renovations, we have enjoyed a surge of interest culminating in the city of Portland and Multnomah County's own One Percent for Public Art Program. Led by Governor Thomas McCall, City Commissioner Mildred Schwab and County Commissioner Earl Blumenauer, other concerned government representatives, citizens and organizations such as Artists Equity urged passage of these important programs, which continue today under the auspices of the Metropolitan Arts Commission and the Oregon Arts Commission.

Concentrating mainly on works visible from outside, this Guide covers but a fraction of the public art that is available for study. Consequently, the works of Carl Morris, C. S. Price, Lucinda Parker and Sally Haley (among a number of fine artists) are not mentioned. A rewarding tour of places rich in art would include the Portland Art Museum, the Oregon Historical Center, the Civic Auditorium, the Pittock Mansion, Kaiser-Permanente Medical Center, commercial art galleries, the headquarters of major corporations and financial institutions, and government offices. Currently, more than 500 works from the Metropolitan Arts Commission's collection circulate through city and county buildings.

While we consider many Portland buildings to be works of art, we leave that subject to other fine regionally published books. (See *Portland: An Informal History and Guide*, Western Imprints, The Press of The Oregon Historical Society, 1984.) Nevertheless, while viewing particular works of art, we began to look up and notice the terra cotta, cast-iron, and carved shells, waves, faces, monsters, flowers and geometrical designs embellishing our city's older buildings. They are clearly cousins, on a much smaller scale, to the city's older works of public art.

In closing, we are pleased to acknowledge the contribution of Mr. James Westhusing. Without his dedicated detective work this Guide could not have been written. We thank him for his time, his patience and his enthusiasm.

PORTLAND'S
PUBLIC
ART

Each number refers to the location of an individual piece or grouping of Portland's public art on the maps and indexes contained in this guide.

The foundry is hot and acrid. As the artist watches, molten bronze flows down runners into a mold and fills the nine-and-a-half-foot high hollow left by the melted, inner wax form. Months earlier, a "thumbnail sketch" was worked into a dozen 10-by-14-inch wax variations, and one of these was selected and enlarged in plaster, then cast in wax. As the bronze cools, a work of art begun a year ago will near completion. Chasing the surface with chisel and mallet, applying a finish and installing the 2,400-pound piece are the artist's last hurdles.

Hilda Morris's completed sculpture now stands at the Sixth Avenue entrance to the Standard Plaza Building (M27). Wordlessly, the *Ring of Time* speaks "the elliptical tides of water and the elliptical tides of rock." Two blocks east, on the grass outside City Hall, stands Portland's oldest work of public art (M32). The petroglyph (a carving on stone) may also tell of moon-pulled tides, but no one knows the meaning of the circles and rippling lines incised by Indians in its Columbia River basalt. Possibly 500 years old, it resembles ancient, carved Irish stones.

Looking back in time, we find works with qualities of craft, color, texture, shape and theme and call these remnants of vanished cultures works of art. As a result, the history of art includes Egyptian bas-reliefs depicting the victories of pharaohs and hippopotamus hunts; Greek bronzes of heroes and athletes; Roman fountains and carved stone busts; paper-thin Chinese bronzes and paintings watercolored on silk; Byzantine

Elk by Roland H. Perry, M39 (OHS Neg. 9550).

mosaics picturing the power of church and state; and Arabic vines, wreaths and rosettes exuberantly decorating wood, metal, terra cotta and glass. Each of these cultures has influenced Portland's public art.

In Europe after the fall of Rome, sculpture was not carved for hundreds of years until the 12th century, when sculptors began to create again, and to sign their work. The reawakening, or Renaissance, which followed was inspired by Greek, Roman, Arab and Chinese art, and eventually swept west, carried to America by immigrants. In Portland, the Renaissance imprint is clearly visible in the *Washington Park Fountain*, which John (Hans) Staehli, a Swiss immigrant and woodcarver, created in the neo-Renaissance style of the 1890s (M99). Cast in iron, the fountain featured four devilish Pans—the pipe-playing, goat-legged Greek god of flocks—and two ornate bowls topped by a small, cast-iron boy modelled after the artist's son, Ralph. Like many works, Staehli's have suffered vicissitudes: every building embellished with his cast-iron ornamentation has been razed, and the fountain's boy has disappeared.

As with much Renaissance art, Frederic Littman's *Farewell to Orpheus*, cast in 1968, has a mythical root (M11). Presented with a lyre by the Greek god Apollo, Orpheus bewitched listeners, and when his wife Eurydice died, braved the underworld to free her. Unhappily, he forgot that he must not look back, and when he did, she was lost forever. A nymph, Littman's Eurydice floats above a circular pool of water. In the myth, water gave her birth and separated her from Orpheus and earth. Another Greek is James Lee Hansen's seven-foot tall *Talos No. 2.* (M60). Last member of an ancient bronze race, Talos defended Crete until, like Achilles, he was fatally wounded in his only weak spot—his ankle. (Pedestrians racing by him to catch a bus on the Mall may have reason to recall his fate.)

Several transit blocks away, Melvin Schuler's *Thor* has the bulky strength of the Scandinavian god of journeys and justice whose thundering hammer echoes above earth (M62). Appropriately, nails rivet the sculpture's copper plates. Viking culture, which gave us democratic assemblies and thousands of common, daily words—among them sun, moon, sky, life, love and child—makes another appearance, this time in northwest Portland. Keith Jellum's bronze *Mimir* portrays the Norse water god and oracle who spoke wisdom even after he was beheaded. (M116).

The two cedar *Caryatids* at the Fifth Avenue entrance to the Pioneer Courthouse were carved 100 years ago in Denmark for the Jacob Kamm Building, which was torn down in 1947 (M58). The *Caryatids* and Norman Taylor's *Kvinneakt* (M53), whose cloak of hair barely conceals her, are rare Portland examples of the female nude. In ancient Greece, India and Rome, where sculptures of male and female nudes abounded, the female may be traced to a Stone Age

Rebecca at the Well by Sculptor Oliver Barrett & Carl Linde, M24 (OHS Neg. 43188).

Totem Pole by Lelooska, M105 (OHS Neg. 69074). Photo by John Bauguess.

source: the "Mother Goddess." Voluptuous, arms extending the fruit of orchard and field, she represented the fertility of woman and earth.

Artist Dimitri Hadzi turned to the earth and found that "the Columbia River Gorge . . . and the memory of the exploratory spirit of adventurers such as Lewis and Clark inspired me to express Man's power over nature." *River Legend* is a 10-foot high, 13-foot wide arch of basalt quarried at Bond Butte. It evokes the Gorge's Bridge of the Gods, a stone arch of Indian legend, and Stonehenge—that circle of immense stones erected in England thousands of years ago (M41).

Tom Hardy also headed to the Columbia Gorge when he wanted to study the devil's club he would create for his panoramic *Oregon Country*, eight screens of forged and welded bronze each weighing approximately 700 pounds (M9). "We got tired of making leaves," says Hardy, who spent an entire year working full-time with three assistants to complete the Portland State University commission. At the Western Forestry Center, Hardy redesigned the garden and waterfall with landscape architect Wallace Kay Huntington, lugged in every rock and forged the bronze *Fish in Pool* (M104). He has created a Noah's Ark of animals in Portland: birds (Ms78,111,142, 156), deer (M119), beaver (M20) and badger (M105). Forehead striped with the stone's grain, the badger was hewn out of a serpentine nude abandoned by a student.

While his artistic ancestors include the Scythians, the Sumerians and the people of Luristan, who worked bronze animals 3,000 years ago, Hardy explains that "the subject is not birds, the subject is metal. Twentieth century sculpture is interested in shape and the spaces between. Natural forces lend themselves to that."

For Pacific Northwest Indians, the subject *was* birds, as well as a host of other animals, which were believed to hold sacred powers. Leaving the perfect duplication of animals to the Creator, Indians attempted to recreate an animal's essence—the slyness of the fox or the wisdom of the owl (M84). The Indians had no word for artist or art, but knew what was skillfully made and magically powerful. The process of creation was as important as the result. Materials, such as a tree, were ritually addressed before carving, and the design was adapted to the natural outline of the wood.

Lelooska—his name means "whittling boy"—carved two totem poles from red cedars whose shafts tower 50 feet (Ms86,105). At the Washington Park Zoo, the industrious beaver, Oregon's state animal, crouches below the indomitable bear, the immortal eagle and the killer whale. At the top, 12-foot wings outstretched, flies the thunderbird. Depending on your background, animals will mean different things. With Lewis and Clark College's *Four Evangelists*, Lelooska reminds us that in the Middle Ages certain animals symbolized saints (M84).

Sacajawea, the wonderful "Bird-Woman," is a historical figure who has entered myth. According to the journals of Lewis and Clark, sent west in 1804 by President Thomas Jefferson to explore the Oregon Country, she "contributed a full man's share to the success of the expedition, besides taking care of her baby." Arranging for their safe passage through Indian territory, collecting edible roots and fruits and courageously rescuing instruments and papers from a flood, she helped assure the nation's claim to the West. One hundred years later, a group of Portland women easily raised the money for her bronze statue (M97). Suffragettes Abigail Scott Duniway and Susan B. Anthony presided over the dedication at the fairgrounds of the Lewis and Clark Centennial Exposition. Hand lifted toward the ocean, Alice Cooper's *Sacajawea* now stands close to Herman MacNeil's *The Coming of the White Man*. The grave Indian chief and the young brave, who extends a branch in a token of peace, symbolically face the east (M96).

People become legends. Burned at the stake in Rouen after leading French armies to miraculous victory over the English in 1429, *Joan of Arc* makes a surprising appearance in Portland (M133). Riding a huge horse and gripping a torn flag, her face bare (Joan believed herself invincible and only reluctantly agreed to body armor), Eugene Fremiet's bronze statue was erected to honor the American doughboys

Simon Benson standing near one of the many drinking fountains he donated to the city, M25 (OHS Neg. OrHi159).

who fought beside the French in World War I. Her twin rides in the Place des Pyramides in Paris.

Theodore Roosevelt is one of those images of power who ride horses above our heads (M18). (Other examples are Rome's *Emperor Marcus Aurelius* and *Charlemagne* who guards Paris's Notre Dame Cathedral.) *Roosevelt* is not mythic in the same way as Raymond Kaskey's *Portlandia*, who grips a trident, classi-

Harvey W. Scott by Gutzon Borglum, M128 (OHS Neg. 69072). Photo by John Bauguess.

cal symbol of water, and bends toward a wreath of wheat, symbol of Portland's agricultural heritage (M31). The 26th president of the United States, Roosevelt hunted with sculptor Phimister Proctor and visited Portland several times—he laid the cornerstones for the Multnomah Athletic Club and the *Lewis and Clark Memorial* (M101).

Standing between the Oregon Historical Center and the Portland Art Museum, Proctor's bronze sculpture, which depicts Roosevelt in his Spanish-American War uniform, is quite different in spirit from the somber *Abraham Lincoln*, who with bowed head walks one block north (M21). Artist George Waters resisted pressure to create a more ebullient president, declaring that this is the Lincoln of the Civil War years. Across the Willamette River, Pompeii Coppini's serene *George Washington* carries his coat and hat under his arm and faces the nation in buckle shoes, waistcoat and ruffles (M148). Today it is refreshing to recall our first president's sage advice: support the arts and the sciences.

These presidential sculptures of the 1920s were created in the heroic-historical tradition. This is a custom which has changed but not disappeared, although a hero like Thomas Jefferson, sculpted for Portland by Carl Bitter, seems hard to come by today (M146). However, in *Civil Rights Era*, one Albina mural created by Isaac Shamsud-Din and five other artists, Martin Luther King strides through kaleidoscopic images of his life-long crusade to achieve black equality (M145). And in *The Crystal Pallets: Defence of Light*, Richard Posner has built a down-to-earth glass picket fence based on electoral themes (M135). Marching across 10 Multnomah County Elections Building windows, the fence is etched with dozens of historical photographs and quotations, including, "Those who cannot remember the past are condemned to repeat it."

D espite a fair amount of rain and nearby rivers and ocean, Portland has a penchant for fountains. The city's first commissioned work of public art was the *Skidmore Fountain*, whose water spills in a curtain around two bronze caryatids who hold aloft the bowl which fills and overflows (M48). The fountain carries on an ancient architectural tradition in which sculptures of the priestesses of Artemis at Caryae became stone caryatids supporting the roofs of Greek temples. But fountains themselves go back even earlier to the sculpted and stepped Assyrian river fountain, which is an ancestor of Bruce West's river sculpture (M139). Today we know that the mythic fountain of life is the fountain of waters which makes a great circle through ocean, air and earth. Still another theme circulates through *The Quest* (M37). Count Alexander von Svoboda's 17-

ton grouping of boys and girls set in a pool of jetting founts represents "the growth of today . . . awakening to the future."

Responding to the past is *Rumi's Dance*, a Jack Youngerman tapestry (M41). The word *dervish* (the Persian *darwish* means doorsill) describes a person on the threshold of enlightenment. Rumi was a 13th century poet-philosopher and the master of the whirling dervishes who, "with a low rustle like a wind before the storm," revolve in two counter-clockwise circles, spinning faster and faster until they stop, streaming with sweat.

A spiritual thread links the tapestry with Don Wilson's *Holon*, meaning "the whole" (M10). The limestone sculpture suggests the unity of body and soul. Quite different is *Narcissus Machine* which brilliantly reflects its moving brass wheel and spokes in a pool of polished glass (M28). Delight in its own mechanical image, suggests artist Will Martin, is the *Machine's* only reason for being. In contrast, natural themes breathe life into Manuel Izquierdo's *Silver Dawn* (M114), Ken Butler's mural of clouds (M115) and Hilda Morris's *Windgate* (M126).

Many religious themes evolved from natural themes. Religious works once dominated public art by virtue of belief and patronage, and they are visible in Portland. More than 100 churches and temples possess stained glass windows whose dark exteriors hint at the warm, unearthly glow within. The city's oldest examples, from 1873, were created in Europe by unknown artists and are among those at Trinity Episcopal Church (M109). The Pioneer Church holds a window, *Crown of Light* (M121), dating from 1889, which was shipped around the Horn, while the Old Church (M14), the First Presbyterian (M76), the First Baptist (M77), and the First Congregational (M22) contain late 19th century windows by David Povey, a Portland artist famous for his use of opalescent glass and sandcast gems, and for his lily motif. Young Albert A. Gerlach went to work for Povey in 1925. His windows can be found throughout the city; his favorite is at Temple Beth Israel (M110). C. Bryce

George Washington by Pompeii Coppini, M148 (OHS Neg. 42320).

Anderson, a local artist working today, learned his art from Gerlach and went on to execute windows at St. James Lutheran (M15), Holy Trinity Greek Orthodox (M134) and more than 20 other churches.

Diverse works of art embody religious themes. They include: Berthold Schiwetz's *St. Francis and His Friends* (M112); the Grotto's 28 linden wood carvings and 15 marble statues (M150); "Buster" Rose's carved relief, *The Last Supper* (M120); Carl Linde's *Shemanski Fountain*, its Biblical *Rebecca at the Well* created by Oliver L. Barrett (M24); and Lee Kelly's *Our Lady Seat of Wisdom* (M8), a bronze Mary with a Byzantine face who is holding flames. Images of violence and suffering permeated Medieval and Renaissance art. In Portland, such works are rare.

Some works of public art appear to enjoy an ambiguous ground, a twilight of meaning. Barbara Hepworth's *Dual Form* (M17) and Clement Meadmore's *Split Ring* (M17) are just that: a dual form and a split ring, but they suggest something else. Just what else is up to us. Richard Serra, for one, is not going to give us a clue. His metal prop work is untitled (M17).

In large part, meaning rests with the viewer. To a two-year-old, *Split Ring* is "a doughnut." To a believer in the occult, the enamel colors and forms fired on John Killmaster's untitled steel plates could carry symbolic significance (M26). Elsewhere, material and technique appear to be the theme. Roy Setziol's carved wood panels mingle intricate natural and geometric shapes in rich teak and have a magnificent reason for existence—to delight the artist and viewer (Ms70,89,120).

Other works of public art simultaneously serve a function. A spectacular example is Ed Carpenter's stained glass which glazes the 30-foot high western wall of the Justice Center (M42). Designed to reflect the building's strong vertical and horizontal patterns and to be seen equally well inside or out, the leaded window mixes beveled pieces, which cast refracted light on the entrance below, with reflective and colored glass.

Less obvious are the sculptures which vent used air (M142), take in fresh air (M2), or serve as a band-

Abraham Lincoln by George Waters, M21 (OHS Neg. 69067). Photo by John Bauguess.

stand shell (M47). Art also finds its way to the threshold of buildings: Jay Wilson's carved wood door at the Yamhill Law Center (M75), Victor (Trader Vic) Bergeron's painted Polynesian doors (M65), A. E. Doyle's elegant entrance to Multnomah County Library (M74) and Avard T. Fairbank's bronze doors at the United States National Bank building which are visible only after the bank closes (M64). Like Ghiberti's 15th century *Gates of Paradise* in Florence and Rodin's *Gates of Hell* in Paris, Fairbank's doors are divided into panels. Inside the panels, intricately carved figures and landscapes symbolize such themes as exploration, settlement and growth and international goodwill.

Parks may be the most familiar yet unrecognized works of functional art. Dedicated to recreation, they are sometimes the result of inspired landscape design.

17

One great illustration is New York City's Central Park, created by Frederick Law Olmsted and Calvert Vaux to unite the natural and the man-made. Another is Portland's *Washington Park* (M94). Commissioned in 1903 to advise on its design, Olmsted's son John urged the city to hold formal plantings to a minimum and save money to buy more land. The result, achieved by artisans working over the last 80 years, is a park of formal plantings, picturesque walks and drives, meadow and wild forest settings.

Within this work of landscape art lies a smaller work. Designed by Professor Takumo P. Tono in 1963, the *Japanese Garden* includes the Sand and Stone Garden—Kare-Sansui—and the carved stone Sapporo Lantern (M95). The *Japanese Garden* eloquently expresses the Pacific Northwest's Oriental heritage. Here, within a landscape art tradition hundreds of years old, religious and philosophical beliefs are tranquilly revealed.

One of public art's most ancient roles is memorial—a physical tribute to the past, to revered individuals and groups of people. *The Soldiers' Monument* salutes the Oregonians who died in the Spanish-American War (M38). The statue of *Harvey W. Scott* by Gutzon Borglum, who sculpted Mount Rushmore and the U.S. Capitol building's Lincoln, pays tribute to the *Oregonian* newspaper's influential 19th century editor (M128). Avard Fairbank's *David Campbell Memorial* is dedicated to the Portland fire chief who rushed into a burning building to help his men and perished. It also honors other city firemen who have died in the line of duty (M80). Lee Kelly's 12-foot tall welded steel sculpture, which stands, surrounded by roses, with immense, cross-beamed dignity, honors Frank E. Beach, an ardent proponent of Portland as the Rose City (M98). Kelly's *Elkhorn*, commissioned by friends, is dedicated to his son, Jason (M119).

United States National Bank Doors by Avard Fairbanks, M64 (OHS Neg. 69075).

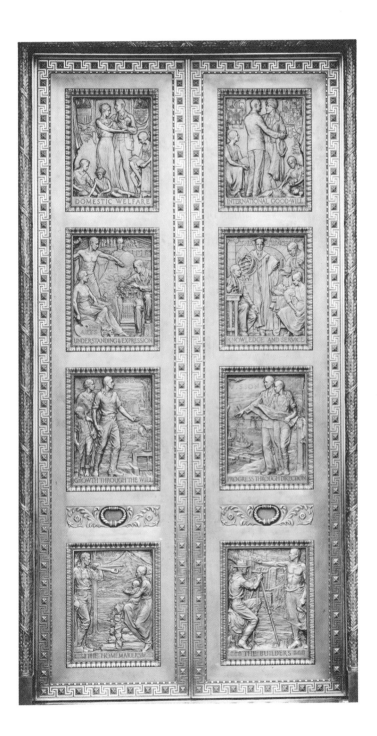

Stephen G. Skidmore (OHS Neg. 9098).

If public art mirrors the past, reflecting the taste and temper of its patrons and times, who made Portland's public art possible? The first patron was Stephen G. Skidmore, a businessman, politician and real estate developer. He arrived at the village of Portland by covered wagon. When his father left for California and did not return, young Stephen peddled milk and delivered newspapers to help support his family. Eventually, he became a druggist, owning his own store and selling patent medicines and fine toilet soaps, as well as artists' materials and fishing rods.

When he was not working, Skidmore visited friends, collected paintings, played the piano and served on the city council and as a volunteer in the fire department. In 1878 he represented Oregon at the Paris World's Fair and made the Grand Tour of Europe. He was particularly impressed by Europe's fountains. Five years later, a millionaire by today's standards, he died of tuberculosis. In his will, he left $5,000 for a fountain where "horses, men, and dogs" could drink.

His business partner, Charles E. Sitton, was joined in the search for the fountain's sculptor by Portland attorney and writer C.E.S. Wood, who supported Sitton's opinion that "in justice to Steve Skidmore and this youthful town, we ought to begin with the very best." Wood warned that $5,000 would not do the fountain justice, and eventually Sitton, with two other Skidmore friends, Henry Failing and Tyler Woodward, anonymously contributed an additional $13,000. Meanwhile Wood had obtained the services of sculptor Olin L. Warner and on September 22, 1888, the Skidmore Fountain, appropriately inscribed "GOOD CITIZENS ARE THE RICHES OF A CITY," was unveiled (M48).

David P. Thompson, another early patron, arrived in Portland at age 19 having driven sheep along the Oregon Trail. He went on to become deputy surveyor, an investor in land, captain of the First Oregon Cavalry in the Civil War, mayor, president of the Humane Society, and minister plenipotentiary and envoy extraordinary to Turkey. In November 1900, he bestowed the bronze *Elk* upon Portland (M39). In an age when water did not gush from every spigot, and plumbing was the exception, he coupled a drinking fountain with a sculpture of the animal which once grazed nearby and over the west hills. Once accused of being an obstacle to traffic, Roland Perry's *Elk* has withstood the charge of many a car and truck.

First chairman of the Oregon Highway Commission, Simon Benson hewed a fortune out of timber, built the Benson Hotel and was instrumental in financing the Columbia River Gorge Highway. A sheepherder in Norway, Benson arrived in Portland in 1879, suffered a series of financial failures and lost his wife to illness. When his luck turned, he declared, "No rich man has the right to die and not leave part of his money to the public." Fortunately, he "wanted the fun of spending my money for the public good while I was still alive."

The result is a number of munificent gifts, including the bronze *Benson Fountains* of 1917 (M25). The 20, four-bowl drinking fountains, given by Benson to slake the thirst of his beer-drinking loggers, as well as 20 additional fountains more recently cast, are located throughout downtown Portland. The fountains were designed by A. E. Doyle, the Portland architect responsible for many fine buildings. (The Multnomah County Library (M74) and the Meier and Frank Building (M59), to name two, are still used for their original purposes.)

In the 1920s, Dr. Henry Waldo Coe enlarged on Portland's tradition of patronage when he established monuments to great men and women which he hoped would serve as an inspiration to the public (Ms21,133). Then, for two decades a hiatus in private giving occurred as the Great Depression and World War II distracted most Americans. But in the 1950s, patronage resumed, and in the last 25 years has become increasingly frequent.

Private donors have contributed the score of sculpted animals at the Washington Park Zoo (M105), Niels Fieldskov's *Wooden Ice Skater* of 1855 (M142), Al Goldsby's *Turtles* (M119), the *Evan H. Roberts Memorial Sculpture Mall* (M17) and many other works of public art. Students and alumni of local schools and colleges have seeded many pieces: Tom Hardy's *Shorebirds Landing* at Lincoln High School (M78), the *Buckman School Mural* (M137), Manuel Izquierdo's work at the University of Portland

The Japanese Gardens, Washington Park, by Dr. Takumo Tono, M95 (OHS Neg. 66571). Photo by Fred DeWolfe.

(M153), and numerous sculptures at Catlin Gabel School (M119).

Portland businesses have increasingly adopted the city's century-old tradition. Among the firms which have funded public art: Standard Insurance Company (M27), the Lloyd Corporation (M142), United States National Bank (M64), Evans Products Company (M23), First Interstate Bank (M29), ESCO (M117), Georgia-Pacific Corporation (M137), Orbanco (Ms34,35,36) and Kaiser-Permanente Medical Centers (M144). Other companies, such as Benson Industries and Cascade Tempering, have contributed labor and materials (M135).

These corporate decisions are made by individuals. David, Mark and Melody Teppola commissioned *Nash*, a 16-foot tall steel sculpture for National Builders Hardware Company because, said Melody, "We

Working in his studio, Frederick Littman places the finishing touches on his sculpture, Joy, M93 (OHS Neg. 66574). Photo courtesy of Marianne Littman.

always dreamed that if we built a new building, we would do it as nicely as possible and incorporate art. Even if some people don't like the sculpture, we hope they appreciate the gesture." (M136).

Pioneer Courthouse Square is a grand gesture made by all the people of Portland in partnership with local businesses, foundations and the federal government (M58). Originally the site of Portland's first schoolhouse and later the magnificent Portland Hotel, the $7.5 million *Square* includes terra cotta columns, an amphitheater and a pergola (a bronze arbor). Paving bricks inscribed with the names of donors confirm the collective effort.

In 1980, the city of Portland and Multnomah County mandated that one percent of public construction budgets for new buildings or renovations would be dedicated to art. Artists throughout the nation have competed for commissions to create works at The Portland Building (M31), Multnomah County Elections Building (M135) and Blue Lake Park (M157). The variety of art at the Justice Center, beginning at Third Avenue and moving through its block-long, public lobbies, is particularly interesting (M42). The Oregon Arts Commission's works at Portland State University resulted from the state's own One Percent for Art Program, while the newly renovated Portland Civic Stadium's steel-sheathed, sculpted ticket booths were paid for by the city of Portland through the Exposition and Recreation Commission (M81).

The federal government has been a patron of the arts for more than a century, and during the Great Depression, a time of desperate need, instituted the Public Works of Art Projects, the Federal Arts Projects of the Works Progress Administration (WPA) and the U.S. Treasury Relief Arts Projects. These agencies sponsored mainly indoor works of art—paintings and murals in schools, libraries and post offices—which emphasized "American scenes." In Oregon, Mount Hood's Timberline Lodge is the superb example of Depression-era public art. George Berry's *Benjamin Franklin* (M127) and John Ballator's St. Johns Post Office mural (M155) are two of Portland's many examples. Gutzon Borglum, sculptor of *Harvey Scott* (M128), gave one reason for the projects in a letter to President Franklin Roosevelt's administrators: "You are not after masterpieces . . . the real success will be in the interest, the human interest, which you will awaken, with color and design, fairytales and history, and what that does to the nation's mind."

More recently, the Comprehensive Employment and Training Act (CETA) helped public and private agencies sponsor art projects (Ms105,139,145,147), while the General Services Administration (GSA)

The *Ira C. Keller Memorial Fountain* by Laurence Halprin & Associates (Angela Danadjieva), M7 (OHS Neg. 69071). Photo by John Bauguess.

Art-in-Architecture program continues to dedicate one half of one percent of estimated federal construction costs to art. (M41) In 1977, Tri-Met and the U.S. Department of Transportation commissioned and sited art on the Portland Mall as part of a larger plan to give new zest to public transportation downtown. Simultaneously, the Portland Development Commission (PDC), using a sensible financial strategy, paid for art with the increased tax revenue generated from renewed areas that the art has helped transform (Ms1,3,4,5,7). Over the years, costs to private patrons and government have varied due to inflation, type of materials, size, site and the reputation of the artist. The *Elk* cost $20,000 (M39); *Theodore Roosevelt*, $40,000 (M18); the Justice Center window, which included glass credits, $69,000 (M42); the *Ira C. Keller Memorial Fountain*, $543,000 (M7).

Running counter to all these undertakings, which tend to emphasize big works of art and a formal selection process, are works of art which have risen spontaneously and unbidden. In 1948, Tom Stefopoulos created a bold series of chalk drawings under the Lovejoy ramp to the Broadway Bridge which survive today (M108).

Luckily, various people and organizations have supported the artist's urge to communicate and create. The vast history of patronage includes prominent examples such as the Catholic Church, a host of despots and aristocrats, and the Republic of Florence, which even as it fought for its life against the Milanese in the 1400s embarked upon a huge public art program. Florence wanted glory and a competitive edge, rulers and artistocrats wanted a record of their personal success and the Church wanted images of religious inspiration and awe. Fine artists fulfilled their patrons' desires while maintaining their own artistic standards.

Artists have always been noted as skilled with their hands (the word "art" comes from the Latin word for skill). Today, artists still work with their hands and the material of earth—clay, sand, wood, stone, metal and fibers. Their techniques are time-tested and varied. Depending simply on earth and a hot kiln, basic ceramic production has not changed significantly since the year 1 A.D., when artists set pieces of ceramic tile in walls, floors, and ceilings to create mosaics. In Portland, Will Martin applied bits of ceramic, including dinnerplates, into concrete to create his Zoo mural (M105). John Rogers used a slip-cast method developed in the 1770s, then fired *A Hundred and Nineteen Modules* to create a ceramic relief for the west wall of the City Parking garage (M72). In a distantly related process, Liz Mapelli cut and stacked pieces of glass and fired them in her kiln until they fused. Her 190-foot long mosaic arcade ceiling at the Justice Center is a harmonious design of rose and gray Venetian glass tiles framing the larger, brilliantly colored, fused glass tiles (M42).

Glass itself is the fusion of sand—silica salts—colored with metals when molten. Working with either rolled glass or handblown antique glass and a soldering iron, Ed Carpenter translated the design for his piece at the Oregon School of Arts and Crafts by joining cut glass shapes with strips of lead (M118). Techniques, including the creation of a full-size pattern, or cartoon, have changed little since the Middle Ages. (Interestingly, stained glass inspired late medieval painters to create with oil paint a kindred luminous quality on canvas.) However, Frederick Heidel uses a process which originated in Holland less than 20 years ago: pieces of antique glass are laminated to create layers of color which resemble colored streams and give the glass a three-dimensional effect (M141).

Wood will crack, but there its similarity to glass ends. Carved for thousands of years, dense, well-seasoned heartwood allows freer carving than stone. Artists like Roy Setziol use clamps to hold the wood in place, then gouges, saws, mallets and chisels to sketch out the shape that is wanted and chip it away. Scrapers, abraders, rasps, files and sandpaper are used for finer detailing and finishing. But even very simple tools will do. Nineteenth century Pacific Northwest Indians used the adze—a cutting tool with a thin arched blade—to carve the Justice Center eagle's big chest and six-foot wings (M42).

Artists who work in stone speak of stone's resistance and stone's liberation. These artists work hard, and they work in fear of destroying the stone's form. They select stones which have a tight flake pattern and a good grain, such as Kathleen Conchuratt's 3½-by-4½-foot limestone for *Cat in Repose* (M55) and Walter Dusenbery's 17-foot tall travertines (M42).

They work with saws, with hard hammer chisels with a soft, flat top, and with points and rasps; their aim is to release the energy in the block of stone. Five hundred years ago, Michelangelo worked alone, switching from right hand to left as he tired. In con-

Farewell to Orpheus by Frederic Littman, M11 (OHS Neg. 69073). Photo by John Bauguess.

Dual Form by Barbara Hepworth, M17 (OHS Neg. 69070). Photo by John Bauguess.

trast, von Svoboda carved carrera marble with 20 Italian assistants (M37), and Dusenbery works in Italy with the same Pietra Santa bottega sculptors who created The Grotto's sculptures and marble reliefs (Ms42,150).

Stone cannot be forced beyond its natural structure. Bronze, a combination of copper and tin, can be totally transformed. At first, copper was used alone and hammered into shape over a wooden armature or skeleton. Four thousand years later, the French employed a similar method to build the Statue of Liberty, and Raymond Kaskey followed suit, substituting metal for wood (M31). At some point, copper mixed with tin was poured in a mold to create a relief over which, like a three-dimensional map, you can run your hand (Ms17,82). To create a sculpture, molten bronze is poured into a cast. With *cire perdu*, the "lost wax" process, the object to be reproduced in bronze is first cast or formed in wax. This is the method employed on all of Portland's older bronzes (M21,148). Frequently melted down for cannon, many bronze sculptures have not survived. (In a fitting reversal, Napoleon's cannon were melted down for the London statue honoring the Duke of Wellington.)

Less ductile than bronze, stainless steel is harder to cast. Frederic Littman's *The Flogger*, which pays tribute to the steel casting industry, may be the world's largest cast steel sculpture (M117). Quite different in kind is David Cotter's Couch Park work (M106) or Lee Kelly's Reed College piece (M126). Engineering concepts are applied to these sculptures, which are constructed, not carved or molded.

For sculptor Tom Hardy, there are two exciting and important moments: "The first is when the idea comes. The second is when I *know* what it is going to look like. Between these two moments may lie days or years of drudgery and hard labor." The hard labor is a given. The result is not.

Some artists attempt to create an image of the physical world. Just as a scientist may restlessly search for the new, an artist may emphasize free investigation. Others feel that their art is an ambassador from their inner feelings to the outer world, or that their work is a physical symbol of something else—the way the rippled, raked sand of the *Japanese Garden* suggests the sea (M95). While all outdoor works of art invite touching, a few are created especially to be felt, and some artists believe that the inner truth of form is revealed by touch, not by sight (M138). Others are primarily interested in what Hilda Morris calls the "initial gesture," the first physical expression of the idea, which she considers essential to the finished work (Ms27,126).

Artists may want a sculpture to resist or to attack its environment, or hope, as does Manuel Izquierdo, that it embodies "beauty, serenity, and love." In every case, they will have great physical difficulties to overcome. Izquierdo worked two years with an assistant to

Aluminum Sculpture by Robert Maki, M56 (OHS Neg. 69068). Photo by John Bauguess.

hammer and weld a 14-foot bronze, worked the metal so lovingly that it shone and not a weld is seen, then filled the sulpture with foam so that rain beats softened to the sound of a kettledrum (M4). Imagine these artists' dismay if, like Olin L. Warner, they arrived in Portland to find the sculpture they planned to install missing. (Frantic telegraphing unearthed the *Skidmore Fountain* in Walla Walla.)

After all this work, artists hope to make a living, but to survive they may have to do something else. If you were skilled enough to be a sculptor, you were skilled enough to be a defense engineer was the 16th century view, and Michelangelo did prove skilled. Against ferocious attack, his defenses held. Today, artists often teach. In Portland, Lee Kelly, Manuel Izquierdo and James Hansen studied with Frederic Littman and Louis Bunce.

Louis Bunce worked with canvas, brushes and paints and always knew that art can be controversial. Portland's *Elk* (M39), was called "a monstrosity of nature" in 1900, and Bunce's Portland International Airport painting roused a storm of debate when, in 1958, it was unveiled (M152). The painting does not resemble a traditional landscape. Its colors and its rectangular shapes suggest a great deal, but decline to be specific. Bunce invites viewers to gather clues, but unlike Sherlock Holmes he never confirms their suspicions. The painting is "abstract," but abstraction is nothing new; it made its first prolific appearance thousands of years ago.

Portland's public art is rooted in ancient and modern traditions from around the world. Morris's bold brushstroke in bronze is linked to the flowing strokes of Japanese Zen painters and calligraphers (M27). Designed by Angela Danadjieva for Lawrence Halprin Associates, the *Ira C. Keller Memorial Fountain*, its 13,000 gallons of water cascading each minute over terraced, concrete platforms, suggests the Northwest landscape and evokes Mayan architecture (M7). Tom Hardy's *Beaver* (M20) and the Albina mural project's *Vanport: the Promise* (M145) recollect elements of regional history.

Isaac Shamsud-Din's Justice Center mural recalls the vivid boiling movement and populist passions painted by Mexican artist Diego Rivera in the 1930s (M42). Steve Gillman's Blue Lake sculpture is linked to the Tibetan practice of placing stones at water sources in homage to the gods and the Chinese and Japanese practice of arranging stones as mountains in gardens (M157). Portland's earliest sculptures were created by Europeans and Americans grounded in the classical 19th century Beaux-Arts. With *Joy*, Hungarian-born sculptor Frederic Littman bridged the classical and modern traditions (M93). In sum, modern art uses Far Eastern, African, pre-Columbian, early Greek or early Christian (Romanesque) traditions as sources. The result may seem exotic or

Frank E. Beach Memorial Fountain by Lee Kelly, M98 (OHS Neg. 69069). Photo by John Bauguess.

strange, but at its best this synthesis does not attempt to create variety for variety's sake. At its best, it is an expanded language used with honesty, charged with feeling.

Because the visual language of artists is based on the physical world we see, art's strength is also its curse: we expect to read its colors and shapes, to understand what they are. If a work of art serves a practical function, it is easier to accept that its colors and patterns, like music's tones and rhythms, can "mean" nothing and still be enjoyed. For this and other reasons, artists and architects have begun to work together again to create buildings which naturally integrate architecture and art.

In Portland, these collaborations are proving increasingly important. In the early fifties, architect Pietro Belluschi followed A. E. Doyle's example

(M64). He commissioned Frederic Littman to execute copper doors (M82). Recently, John Storrs (Ms104,118), Zimmer, Gunsul, Frasca (M42), Skidmore, Owings and Merrill (M27) and Fletcher, Finch and Farr (Ms85,113) have continued this tradition. The Portland Performing Arts Center, designed by Broome, Oringdulph, O'Toole, Rudolf and Associates, the ELS Design Group and Barton Myers Associates, promises to be the rare example of architects and artists working together from a project's inception (M23).

Artists often collaborate with each other. Bonnie Bronson, a sculptor in her own right (M42), enamelled Lee Kelly's sculpture *Leland I* (M1); students at Duniway School and the University of Portland helped construct Kelly pieces (Ms123,153); students and members of the Northwest Neighborhood Association worked on Jere Grimm's Couch Park mosaics (M107); Gloria Ross wove Jack Youngerman's tapestry (M41). Parallel to a medieval community building a cathedral, private citizens, artists, architects, local business and government invested years of effort creating *Pioneer Courthouse Square* (M58).

Portland is both a place which is given and a city that is being made. The river which divides the valley, the mountains which surround it, the quality of light and the climate are given. The parks, streets, buildings, bridges and art are made, and given to future generations. But much that is made vanishes. The original setting for the *Skidmore Fountain* was a "six-sided plaza, cobbled in Belgian block, Florentine and Baroque facades set like screens around it, . . . the plaza's fine streets leading off in long . . . vistas of classical arcades." Today only a few buildings and the *Fountain* remain (M48). Without the championship of Francis Murname, head of the Longshoreman's Union, and some dedicated citizens, the *Skidmore Fountain*, the *Shemanski Fountain* (M24), *Joan of Arc* (M133) and the *Benson Fountains* (M25) would be rubble. Our roots can be uprooted.

Artist Isaac Shamsud-Din stands in front of one of his Albina murals, M145 (OHS Neg. 69902). Photo by John Bauguess.

The works of public art commissioned today are connected to those roots and reach out toward new territory. Scott McIntire's *Zoo Bus*, Portland's first transporting work of public art, which plies a route between Washington Park and downtown, would have been unimaginable in the past (M103). Hap Tivey's *Portland Portrait* is called a painting, but its canvas is aluminum and its paint is argon light (M45). David Cotter's *Pod 48* is one of the nation's few outdoor kinetic sculptures (M119). Entering new territory, these and other works share the Northwest heritage of exploration and discovery—an appreciation for the search as well as its reward. These themes are central to the history of the region and to the history of art.

A true work of art persists as an object of contemplation. It may not be "beautiful," it may at times be forgotten, but it always invites thought and reflection. When we look at a work of art and respond, it is a tribute not only to the artist, but to us. As the old proverb says, "A good spectator also creates."

SUGGESTED FURTHER READING

Clere, Bruce and Portland Public Schools Art Department. *Art in the Community*. (unpublished manuscript).

Griffin, Rachael, and Donald Jenkins. *Paintings and Sculptures of the Pacific Northwest*. Portland: Portland Art Museum, 1959.

Griffin, Rachael, and Martha Kingsbury. *Art of the Pacific Northwest: From the 1930s to the Present*. Washington, D.C.: Smithsonian Institution Press, 1974.

Kingsbury, Martha. *Northwest Traditions*. Seattle: Seattle Art Museum, 1978.

McCarthy, Bridget Beattie. *Architectural Crafts*. Seattle: Madrona Press, 1982.

O'Donnell, Terence, and Thomas Vaughan. *Portland: An Informal History and Guide*. Portland: Western Imprints, The Press of The Oregon Historical Society, 1984.

Snyder, Eugene E. *Skidmore's Portland, His Fountain and Its Sculptor*. Portland: Binfords and Mort, 1973.

Taylor, Joshua C. *America As Art*. New York: Harper & Row, 1979.

INDEX I
NUMERICAL

Each number refers to the location of an individual piece or grouping of Portland's public art on the maps contained in this guide.

1
Kelly, Lee (Assisted by David Cotter and Bonnie Bronson)
LELAND #1
Sculpture—Steel and Enamel
1975
Commission of Portland Development Commission
S.W. 2nd and Lincoln

2
Walker, Peter (Assisted by Zimmer, Gunsul, Frasca)
UNTITLED
Landscape Garden and Brick Sculpture
1974
Commission of Pacific Northwest Bell Telephone Company
S.W. 4th and College

3
Lawrence Halprin and Associates
LOVEJOY FOUNTAIN
Sculpture and Fountain—Concrete
1966
Commission of Portland Development Commission
Portland Center, S.W. Hall

4
Izquierdo, Manuel
THE DREAMER
Sculpture—Bronze
1979
Commission of Portland Development Commission
Pettygrove Park, S.W. 3rd between Market and Harrison

5
Senft, Douglas
AWNING
Sculpture—Aluminum
1976
Commission of Portland Development Commission
S.W. 3rd and Market

6
Civic Auditorium
Numerous paintings and sculptures
Commission of City and County and private donations.
S.W. 3rd and Clay

7
Lawrence Halprin and Associates (Angela Danadjieva)
IRA C. KELLER MEMORIAL FOUNTAIN
Sculpture and Fountain—Concrete
1971
Commission of Portland Development Commission
S.W. 3rd and Clay

8
Kelly, Lee
OUR LADY SEAT OF WISDOM
Sculpture—Bronze and Enamel
1965
Commission of St. Mary's High School
1615 S.W. 5th

9
Hardy, Tom
OREGON COUNTRY
Sculpture/Screen—Bronze
1962
Commission of Portland State
University
Neuberger Hall
724 S.W. Harrison

10
Hepburn, Tony
UNTITLED
Sculpture—Stone
1983
Commission of Portland State
University, National
Endowment for the Arts,
Metropolitan Arts Commission
South Park Blocks at Harrison

10
Wilson, Don
HOLON "THE WHOLE"
Sculpture—Indiana Limestone
1979
Commission of Portland State
University Foundation in Memory
of Dr. Gordon Hearn
S.W. Hall and Park

11
Littman, Frederic
FAREWELL TO ORPHEUS
Sculpture—Bronze
1973
Gift of William Roberts, Hall
Templeton, the Autzen
Foundation, the Collins
Foundation and the Portland
Development Commission
Portland State University
South Park Blocks at Montgomery

12
Heidel, Frederick
ALL IN A ROW
Sculpture—Glass
1969
Commission of Portland State
University
Science 1 Building
1025 S.W. Mill

13
Brownlee, Edward
RAINBOW TREE
Sculpture—Aluminum
1980
Purchase of Jordan Schnitzer
Clay Tower Apartments
1430 S.W. 12th

14
Povey, David
WINDOWS
Stained Glass
Late 19th or early 20th century
Commission of Calvary
Presbyterian Church
The Old Church
1422 S.W. 11th

15
Anderson, C. Bryce
WINDOWS
Stained Glass
1982
Commission of St. James
Lutheran Church
1315 S.W. Park

15a
Gillman, Steve
UNTITLED
Sculpture—Granite
1984
Commission of City of Portland
and National Park Service
South Park Blocks between S.W.
Columbia and Jefferson

15b
Sutinen, Paul
UNTITLED
Environmental Sculpture—
Granite
1984
Commission of City of Portland
and National Park Service
South Park Blocks between S.W.
Market and Clay

16
Kosuge, Michihiro
UNTITLED
Sculpture—Steel
1972
Gift of Tom Hardy
Portland Art Museum
1219 S.W. Park

17
Belluschi, Pietro and
Wolff, Zimmer, Gunsul, Frasca
and Ritter, Architects
EVAN H. ROBERTS
MEMORIAL SCULPTURE
MALL
Mall—Brick
1970
Gift of the Roberts Family
Portland Art Museum
1219 S.W. Park

17
Hepworth, Barbara
DUAL FORM
Sculpture—Bronze
1965
Purchase by Museum Building
Fund and the Dayton Hudson
Corporation Foundation
Portland Art Museum, Evan H.
Roberts Memorial Sculpture Mall
1219 S.W. Park

17
Kelly, Lee
ARLIE
Sculpture—Steel
1978
Loan from the Artist
Portland Art Museum, Evan H.
Roberts Memorial Sculpture Mall
1219 S.W. Park

17
Meadmore, Clement
SPLIT RING
Sculpture—Steel
1969
Purchase by the Roberts Memorial
Sculpture Collection Fund
Portland Art Museum, Evan H.
Roberts Memorial Sculpture Mall
1219 S.W. Park

17
Renoir, Pierre Auguste
PORTRAIT OF RODIN
Relief—Bronze
1917
Gift of Walter P. Chrysler
Portland Art Museum, Evan H.
Roberts Memorial Sculpture Mall
1219 S.W. Park

17
Serra, Richard
UNTITLED
Sculpture—Steel
1969
Purchase by the Roberts Memorial
Sculpture Collection Fund
Portland Art Museum, Evan H.
Roberts Memorial Sculpture Mall
1219 S.W. Park

18
Procter, Phimister
THEODORE ROOSEVELT,
ROUGH RIDER
Sculpture—Bronze
1922
Gift of Dr. Henry Waldo Coe
South Park Blocks between
Jefferson and Madison

19
Garnet, William
HORSE CAVALCADE
Mural—Paint on Cinderblock
1982
Commission of the Oregon
Historical Society
Oregon Historical Center
S.W. Park and Madison

20
Hardy, Tom
BEAVER
Sculpture—Bronze
1970
Gift of C. M. Bishop Family in
memory of Thomas K. Sammons
Oregon Historical Center
1230 S.W. Park

21
Waters, George
ABRAHAM LINCOLN
Sculpture—Bronze
1926
Gift of Dr. Henry Waldo Coe
South Park Blocks between Main
and Madison

22
Povey, David
WINDOWS
Stained Glass
Late 19th or early 20th century
Commission of the First
Congregational Church
1126 S.W. Park

23
Portland Performing Arts Center
1984-85
Works of Art
Commissions of City of Portland
One Percent for Public Art
(Metropolitan Arts Commission)
S.W. Broadway and Main

24
Barrett, Oliver and Linde, Carl
REBECCA AT THE WELL
Sculpture and Fountain—Bronze
and Sandstone
1926
Gift of Joseph Shemanski
South Park Blocks between
Salmon and Main

25
Doyle, A. E.
DRINKING FOUNTAINS (20)
Fountains—Bronze
1917
Gift of Simon Benson
Throughout downtown Portland

26
Killmaster, John
UNTITLED
Sculpture—Steel and Porcelain
1977
Commission of Tri-Met and U.S.
Department of Transportation
Transit Mall, S.W. 6th between
Madison and Main

27
Morris, Hilda
RING OF TIME
Sculpture—Bronze
1967
Commission of Skidmore, Owings
& Merrill and Standard Insurance
Company
Standard Plaza, S.W. 6th
between Main and Madison

28
Martin, Willard
NARCISSUS MACHINE
Sculpture—Brass
1962
Commission of Portland Federal
Savings and Loan Association
Standard Plaza
S.W. 5th and Main

29
Changing Exhibits
First Interstate Bank Lobby
Objects from the Bank's Art
Collection
1300 S.W. 5th

30
Wilson, Don
INTERLOCKING FORMS
Sculpture—Indiana Limestone
1977
Commission of Tri-Met and U.S.
Department of Transportation
Transit Mall, S.W. 5th between
Madison and Main

31
Kaskey, Raymond
PORTLANDIA
Sculpture—Copper on Bronze
and Steel Armature
1984
Commission of City of Portland,
Multnomah County One Percent
for Public Art (Metropolitan Arts
Commission)
The Portland Building
1120 S.W. 5th

32
Oregon Country Indians
PETROGLYPH
Carving—Basalt
Ca. 1500 AD (Dedicated in
Portland in 1940)
Gift to the City from the
Geological Society of Oregon
Portland City Hall
1220 S.W. 5th

33
McShane Bell Foundry
LIBERTY BELL
Bell—Bronze
1964
Purchase by City of Portland
S.W. 4th between Jefferson and
Madison

34
Unknown Artist and Skidmore,
Owings & Merrill
ORBANCO GAZEBO
Reconstruction of Window
Arches from Congress Hotel
(Razed in 1978) Dedicated 1982
Commission of Orbanco
Corporation
S.W. 6th and Main

35
Kirkland, Larry
WAVE
Sculpture—Cotton Webbing and
Cast Ceramic Weights by John
Rogers
1978
Commission of Orbanco
Corporation
1001 S.W. 5th

36
Benson, Fletcher
FOLDED CIRCLE BLUE LINE
Sculpture—Stainless Steel
1980
Purchase by Orbanco Corporation
1001 S.W. 5th

37
Coleman, Candace
UNTITLED
Tapestry—Wool and Linen
1979
Commission of Georgia-Pacific
Corporation
900 S.W. 5th

37
Von Svoboda, Count Alexander
PERPETUITY
Sculpture—Wood and Bronze
1970
Commission of Georgia-Pacific
Corporation
900 S.W. 5th

37
Von Svoboda, Count Alexander
THE QUEST
Sculpture—Marble
1970
Commission of Georgia-Pacific
Corporation
900 S.W. 5th

37
West, Bruce
UNTITLED
Sculpture—Steel
1973
Commission of Georgia-Pacific
Corporation
900 S.W. 5th (Lower Level)

38
Tilden, Douglas
SECOND OREGON
COMPANY VOLUNTEERS
Fountain—Limestone and Bronze
1914
Commission of the "Mothers,
Sisters, and Wives" in Honor of
Service May 15, 1898–August 7,
1899 in the Philippines
Lownsdale Square, S.W. 4th
between Main and Salmon

38
Tilden, Douglas and Wright,
H.D.
SOLDIERS' MONUMENT
(Spanish American War)
Sculpture—Bronze
1906
Gift of Citizens of Oregon
Lownsdale Square, S.W. 4th
between Main and Salmon

39
Perry, Roland
ELK
Sculpture—Bronze
1900
Gift of David P. Thompson
S.W. Main between 3rd and 4th

40
Bixel, J. E.
MAYOR TERRY D. SCHRUNK
Plaque—Bronze
1977
Commission of the City of
Portland
Terry D. Schrunk Plaza, S.W. 3rd
between Madison and Jefferson

40
Robert Perron Partnership
MAYOR TERRY D. SCHRUNK
PLAZA
Plaza
1977
Commission of the City of
Portland
S.W. 3rd between Madison and
Jefferson

41
Hadzi, Dimitri
RIVER LEGEND
Sculpture—Basalt
1976
Commission of the U.S. General
Services Administration
Edith Green-Wendall Wyatt
Federal Building
1220 S.W. 3rd

41
Youngerman, Jack (designer) and
Ross, Gloria (weaver)
RUMI'S DANCE
Weaving
1976
Commission of the U.S. General
Services Administration
Edith Green-Wendell Wyatt
Federal Building
1220 S.W. 3rd

42
Bronson, Bonnie
UNTITLED
Sculpture—Enamelled Steel
1983
Commission of U.S. Department
of Transportation, the City of
Portland and Multnomah County
One Percent for Public Art
(Metropolitan Arts Commission,
Oregon Department of
Transportation)
Justice Center
S.W. 3rd and Main

42
Carpenter, Ed
UNTITLED
Stained Glass
1983
Commission of U.S. Department
of Transportation, the City of
Portland and Multnomah County
One Percent for Public Art
(Metropolitan Arts Commission,
Oregon Department of
Transportation)
Justice Center
S.W. 3rd and Main

42
Dusenbery, Walter
UNTITLED
Sculptures—Travertine
1983
Commission of U.S. Department
of Transportation, the City of
Portland and Multnomah County
One Percent for Public Art
(Metropolitan Arts Commission,
Oregon Department of
Transportation)
Justice Center
S.W. 3rd and Main

42
Kwakiutal Indian
PACIFIC NORTHWEST
INDIAN EAGLE
Sculpture—Cedar
19th Century (Installed October
1983)
Purchase of U.S. Department of
Transportation, the City of
Portland and Multnomah County
One Percent for Public Art
(Metropolitan Arts Commission,
Oregon Department of
Transportation)
Justice Center
S.W. 3rd and Main

42
Mapelli, Liz
UNTITLED
Mosaic—Venetian and Fused
Glass Arcade Ceiling
1983
Commission of U.S. Department
of Transportation, the City of
Portland and Multnomah County
One Percent for Public Art
(Metropolitan Arts Commission,
Oregon Department of
Transportation)
Justice Center
S.W. 3rd and Main

42
Shamsud-Din, Isaac
UNTITLED
Mural—Paint on Wood
1983
Commission of U.S. Department
of Transportation, the City of
Portland and Multnomah County
One Percent for Public Art
(Metropolitan Arts Commission,
Oregon Department of
Transportation)
Justice Center
S.W. 3rd and Main

43
Van Hevelingen, Frances
UNTITLED
Painting—Encaustic on Canvas
1980
Commission of Melvin Mark
Properties
Columbia Square Building
111 S.W. Columbia

44
Kenworthy, Bart
BENJAMIN FRANKLIN
Sculpture—Wood
1976
Commission of Benjamin
Franklin Savings and Loan
Association
S.W. Columbia and 1st

45
Tivey, Hap
PORTLAND PORTRAIT
Painting—Aluminum, Argon
Light, Gold Leaf, Acrylic and Oil
1982
Commission of Smith-Ritchie
Company
811 S.W. Front

46
Jensen, Eric and Matsler, Riley
THE WEB OF NEWSPRINT
Sculpture—Concrete
1970 (Removed, 1983)
Commission of the Auld Lang
Syne Society
S.W. 1st and Morrison

47
West, Bruce
UNTITLED
Sculpture—Steel
1978
Commission of Portland
Development Commission
Waterfront Park
S.W. Front and Ash

48
Warner, Olin L.
SKIDMORE FOUNTAIN
Sculpture and Fountain—Bronze
and Granite
1888
Gift of Stephen G. Skidmore,
Charles E. Sitton, Henry Failing
and Tyler Woodward
S.W. 1st and Ankeny

49
Erceg, Joe
BUTTERFLY
Mural—Paint on Brick
1976
Commission of Norcrest China
Company
S.W. 1st and Davis

50
Kelly, Lee
UNTITLED
Sculpture and Fountain—Steel
1977
Commission of Tri-Met and U.S.
Department of Transportation
Transit Mall, S.W. 6th between
Pine and Ankeny

50
Carter, Hull, Nishita, McCulley
and Baxter
UNTITLED
Fountain—Steel and Concrete
1977
Commission of Tri-Met and U.S.
Department of Transportation
Transit Mall, S.W. 5th and
Ankeny

51
Kelly, Charles
MATRIX III
Sculpture—Steel and Concrete
1977
Commission of Tri-Met and U.S.
Department of Transportation
Transit Mall, S.W. 6th between
Stark and Oak

52
West, Bruce
UNTITLED
Sculpture—Steel
1977
Commission of Tri-Met and U.S.
Department of Transportation
Transit Mall, S.W. 5th between
Stark and Oak

53
Taylor, Norman
KVINNEAKT "Nude Woman"
Sculpture—Bronze
1977
Commission of Tri-Met and U.S.
Department of Transportation
Transit Mall, S.W. 5th and
Washington

54
Beardlee, Bridge
FORMS FOUND IN NATURE
AND IN THE TOOLS OF MEN
Sculpture—Aluminum (Fountain
designed by William Berkey)
1972
Commission of Portland Federal
Savings and Loan Association
S.W. 5th and Washington

55
Conchuratt, Kathleen
CAT IN REPOSE
Sculpture—Indiana Limestone
1977
Commission of Tri-Met and the
U.S. Department of
Transportation
Transit Mall, S.W. 5th between
Alder and Morrison

56
Maki, Robert
UNTITLED
Sculpture and Fountain—
Aluminum and Stone
1977
Commission of Tri-Met and U.S.
Department of Transportation
Transit Mall, S.W. 6th between
Taylor and Yamhill

57
Carter, Hull, Nishita, McCulley
and Baxter
UNTITLED
Fountain—Granite
1977
Commission of Tri-Met and the
U.S. Department of
Transportation
Transit Mall, S.W. 5th and
Yamhill

58
Martin, Willard and Associates
(Terence O'Donnell, Robert
Reynolds, Spencer Gill, Lee Kelly
and Douglas Macy)
PIONEER COURTHOUSE
SQUARE
Park—Brick and Concrete
1983
Gifts of the Citizens of Portland,
Foundations and Corporations
and Grants from the City of
Portland and the U.S.
Government
S.W. 6th between Yamhill and
Morrison

58
Unknown Artist
CARYATIDS
Sculpture—Wood
1884
Carved in Denmark for the Jacob
Kamm building
Pioneer Court House, S.W. 6th
between Yamhill and Morrison

59
Doyle, A. E. and Associates
Meier and Frank Building
1904 (Additions 1915, 1930)
Commission of Meier and Frank
Company
621 S.W. 5th

60
Hansen, James Lee
TALOS NO. 2
Sculpture—Bronze
1977
Commission of Tri-Met and U.S.
Department of Transportation
Transit Mall, S.W. 6th between
Morrison and Alder

61
Morrison, Ivan
UNTITLED
Sculpture—Aluminum
1977
Commission of Tri-Met and U.S.
Department of Transportation
Transit Mall, S.W. 6th between
Washington and Alder

62
Schuler, Melvin
THOR
Sculpture—Copper on Redwood
1977
Commission of Tri-Met and the
U.S. Department of
Transportation
Transit Mall, S.W. 5th between
Alder and Washington

63
Schuler, Melvin
UNTITLED
Sculpture—Copper on Redwood
Ca. 1975
Purchase by Far West Federal
Savings
Commonwealth Building
421 S.W. 6th

63
Setziol, Monica
UNTITLED
Handwoven Tapestry
Ca. 1975
Purchase by Far West Federal
Savings
Commonwealth Building
421 S.W. 6th

64
Fairbanks, Avard
DOORS
Sculpture—Bronze Relief
1931
Commission of United States
National Bank of Oregon
S.W. Broadway and S.W. 6th and
Stark

64
Carter, Hull, Nishita, McCulley
and Baxter
UNTITLED
Fountain—Granite and Brick
1977
Commission of Tri-Met and the
U.S. Department of
Transportation
Transit Mall, S.W. 6th between
Washington and Stark

65
Bergeron, Victor
POLYNESIAN DOORS
Doors—Carved and Painted
Wood
1959
Gift of the Artist
Trader Vic's
S.W. Broadway and Stark

66
Demetriades
UNTITLED
Sculpture and Fountain—Bronze
and Concrete
1970
Commission of Bank of California
707 S.W. Washington

67
Kelly, Lee
UNTITLED
Sculpture—Steel
1977
Purchase by Pacific Northwest
Bell Telephone Company
310 S.W. Park

68
Unknown Artist
FEMALE FIGURES FLOATING
Sculptures—Wood
Ca. 1620
Purchase by William Roberts for
the Morgan Building
720 S.W. Washington

69
Danile, Mann, Johnson and
Mendenhall
O'BRYANT SQUARE
Park and Fountain
1973
Gift of William Roberts, the
Sloan Foundation and the
Portland Rose Society and Grants
from the City of Portland and the
U.S. Government
S.W. Park and Washington

70
Setziol, LeRoy
UNTITLED
Relief—Teak
1970
Commission of Farwest Life
Insurance Company
812 S.W. Washington

71
West, Bruce
UNTITLED
Sculpture—Steel
1976
Commission of the Gilley
Company (Cushman &
Wakefield, Inc.)
The Pittock Block
921 S.W. Washington

72
Rogers, John
A HUNDRED AND NINETEEN
MODULES
Relief—Slip-cast Ceramic
1979
Commission of U.S.
Comprehensive Employment and
Training Act
City Parking Garage
S.W. 10th and Yamhill

73
Brown, Greg
BIGHORN SHEEP
Mural—Paint on Concrete
1981
Commission of Mayfield
Investment Company
Medical Arts Building
S.W. 10th and Salmon

74
Doyle, A. E. and Associates
DOORS
1913
Commission of Multnomah
County
Multnomah County Library
801 S.W. 10th Ave.

75
Wilson, Jay
DOOR
Relief—Wood
Year Unknown
Yamhill Law Center
1123 S.W. Yamhill

76
Povey, David
WINDOWS
Stained Glass
Late 19th or early 20th century
Commission of the First
Presbyterian Church
1200 S.W. Alder

77
Gerlach, Albert A.
WINDOWS
Stained Glass
1894
Commission of the First Baptist
Church
909 S.W. 11th

77
Povey, David
WINDOWS
Stained Glass
Late 19th or early 20th century
Commission of the First Baptist
Church
909 S.W. 11th

78
Hardy, Tom
SHORE BIRDS LANDING
Sculpture—Bronze
1960
Gift of Judge Otto J. Kraemer
Lincoln High School
1600 S.W. Salmon

79
Gardiner, James
THE AUDIENCE
Mural—Paint on Wood
1976
Commission of Portland Civic
Theater
1530 S.W. Yamhill

80
Fairbanks, Avard and
Tucker, E. F.
DAVID CAMPBELL
MEMORIAL
Sculpture and Fountain—Kozota
Stone and Bronze
1928
Gift of Portland Citizens in
Memory of Captain
David Campbell and Other
Firemen Killed in Action
S.W. 19th and Burnside

81
West, Bruce
TICKET BOOTHS
Sculpture—Steel
1982
Commission of City of Portland
Civic Stadium
S.W. 18th and Morrison

82
Littman, Frederic
DOORS
Relief—Copper
1950
Commission of Zion Lutheran
Church
S.W. Salmon and 18th

83
Butterfield, Raleigh C.
THE TECHNOLOGIES
Sculpture—(Mobiles)—Wood,
Plastic, Stainless Steel,
Photography, Human Skeleton
1975
Commission of Amo De Bernerdis
Portland Community College
Sylvania Campus
12000 S.W. 49th

83
Kelly, Lee
UNTITLED
Sculpture—Steel
1972
Purchase by Portland Community
College
12000 S.W. 49th

84
Unknown Artist
DOLPHINS
Sculpture—Bronze
Ca. 1920
From the Estate of Aaron Frank
Lewis and Clark College
0615 S.W. Palatine Hill

84
Lelooska
FOUR EVANGELISTS
Sculptures—Concrete
1969
Gift of Private Donors
Lewis and Clark College
0615 S.W. Palatine Hill

84
Lelooska
OWL
Sculpture—Concrete
1969
Gift of Private Donors
Lewis and Clark College
0615 S.W. Palatine Hill

84
Simonis, Obie
CODA PHYLOGENY
Sculpture—Stainless Steel
1979
Gift of Private Donors
Lewis and Clark College
0615 S.W. Palatine Hill

85
Balazs, Harold
UNTITLED
Sculpture—Cast Concrete
1976
Commission of First State Bank
Pacific Western Bank
S.W. 24th and Barbur

86
Lelooska
TOTEM POLE
Sculpture—Wood
1959
Commission of City of Portland
5700 S.W. Terwilliger

87
Shores, Ken
ALLIUM
Relief—Stoneware
1959
Gift of Artist
Contemporary Crafts Association
3934 S.W. Corbett

88
Jellum, Keith
WINDSHIP
Sculpture—Bronze
1975
Purchase of Tom Walsh
4126 S.W. Corbett

89
Setziol, LeRoy
UNTITLED
Relief—Teak
1970
Commission of Oregon Health
Sciences University
Crippled Children's Division
3181 S.W. Sam Jackson Park Rd.

90
Crutcher, Lewis
FOUNTAIN
Fountain—Marble
1963
Gift of Alumni Association for
the Medical School's 75th
Anniversary
Oregon Health Sciences
University
3181 S.W. Sam Jackson Park Rd.

91
West, Bruce
UNTITLED
Sculpture—Steel
1976
Commission of City of Portland
Art in Public Places Program
(Metropolitan Arts Commission)
Lair Hill Park
3037 S.W. 2nd

92
McKenzie, Dr. Robert Tait
BOY SCOUT (Replica)
Sculpture—Bronze
1937 (Original, 1915)
Gift of Zenon C. R. Hanson
2145 S.W. Front

93
Littman, Frederic
JOY (PIONEER WOMAN)
Sculpture—Bronze
1956
Gift of Mrs. Florence Laberee
Council Crest Park
Top of S.W. Council Crest

94
Olmsted, John and
Portland Park Bureau
WASHINGTON PARK
Landscaping
1904
Commission of Portland Parks
and Recreation Bureau
Washington Park

95
Tono, Dr. Takumo
THE JAPANESE GARDEN
Landscape Garden
1964
Gift of Members and Friends of
the Japanese Garden Society of
Oregon
Washington Park
S.W. Kingston

96
MacNeil, Herman A.
COMING OF THE WHITE
MAN
Sculpture—Bronze
1904
Gift of David P. Thompson
Washington Park

97
Cooper, Alice
SACAJAWEA
Sculpture—Bronze
1905
Commission of Portland Women
for Lewis and Clark
Centennial Exposition
Washington Park

98
Kelly, Lee (assisted by David
Cotter)
FRANK E. BEACH MEMORIAL
FOUNTAIN
Sculpture and Fountain—Steel
1975
Commission of City of Portland,
Frank L. Beach and Estate of Ruth
B. Mehlin
International Rose Test Gardens
Washington Park

99
Staehli, John (Hans)
WASHINGTON PARK
FOUNTAIN
Fountain—Cast Iron
1891
Commission of City of Portland
Washington Park

100
Lavare, Gabriel
LIONS
Relief—Marble
1908
Commission of the City of
Portland for the Lewis and Clark
Memorial
S.W. Park Place and Lewis and
Clark Circle

101
Schumann, Otto
LEWIS AND CLARK
MEMORIAL COLUMN
Sculpture and Plaques—Stone
and Bronze
1908
Commission of the City of
Portland in Honor of the Lewis
and Clark Expedition, Henry
Walton Goode and Henry
Winslow Corbett (Presidents of
the Lewis and Clark Centennial
Exposition)
S.W. Park Place and Lewis and
Clark Circle

102
Doyle, A. E. and Associates
LOYAL B. STEARNS
MEMORIAL FOUNTAIN
Fountain—Marble and Bronze
1936
Gift of Judge Loyal B. Stearns
2400 W. Burnside

103
McIntire, Scott
ZOO BUS
Mural on Bus #63
1982
Commission of the Washington
Park Zoo, OMSI, Western
Forestry Center and Tri-Met
Travels between Downtown and
the Zoo, OMSI and Western
Forestry Center

104
Hardy, Tom and
Huntington, Wallace Kay
FISH IN POOL
Sculpture and Fountain
1975
Commission of Western Forestry
Center
4033 S.W. Canyon

104
Storrs, Anne
UNTITLED
Bench—Tilework
1980
Commission of Western Forestry
Center
4033 S.W. Canyon

105
Bufano, Beniamino
BEAR AND NURSING CUBS
Sculpture—Marble
1978
Gift of Herbert Frybarger and
Sharon Bliss
Washington Park Zoo
4001 S.W. Canyon

105
Giltner, Peter
AFRICAN SCENE
Mural
1978
Commission of U.S.
Comprehensive Employment and
Training Act
Washington Park Zoo
4001 S.W. Canyon

105
Goldsby, Al
TURTLE AND LOG
Sculpture—Bronze
1978
Gift of Mrs. Christine Swigert
Mr. and Mrs. William Roberts
Mr. and Mrs. Howard Vollum
Mr. and Mrs. Eino Kiander
Mr. Maurie Clark
Washington Park Zoo
4001 S.W. Canyon

105
Hardy, Tom
SLEEPING BADGER
Sculpture—Serpentine
1978
Gift of Charlie and Janet
Mersereau and Mrs. Catherine
Piper
Washington Park Zoo
4001 S.W. Canyon

105
Lelooska
TOTEM POLE
Sculpture—Wood
1959
Gift of Douglas Aircraft
Corporation
Washington Park Zoo
4001 S.W. Canyon

54

105
Martin, Willard
THE CONTINUITY OF LIFE
FORMS
Mural—Tile
1959
Commission of the Portland Zoo
Washington Park Zoo
4001 S.W. Canyon

105
Procter, Phimister
LION
Sculpture—Bronze
1911
Loan from the Portland Art
Museum
Washington Park Zoo
4001 S.W. Canyon

105
Smith, Joelle
ELEPHANTS
Mural
1977
Commission of U.S.
Comprehensive Employment and
Training Act
Washington Park Zoo
4001 S.W. Canyon

106
Gibson, John and Jennings, John
A WEEK IN THE LIFE
Mural—Paint on Concrete
1982
Commission of Goose Hollow
Foothills League and Portland
Bureau of Parks and Recreation
S.W. 18th between Mill and
Market

107
Cotter, David
UNTITLED
Sculpture—Steel
1976
Commission of Northwest District
Association, Portland
Development Commission and
U.S. Department of Housing and
Urban Development
Couch Park
N.W. 19th and Glisan

107
Grimm, Jere
UNTITLED
Mosaics—Tile
1976
Commission of U.S.
Comprehensive Employment and
Training Act
Couch Park
N.W. 19th and Glisan

107
Moore, William
UNTITLED
Sculpture—Carved Wooden
Posts
1976
Commission of Northwest District
Association, Portland
Development Commission and
U.S. Department of Housing and
Urban Development
Couch Park
N.W. 19th and Glisan

108
Stefopoulos, Tom
FIGURES AND PHRASES
Drawings—Chalk on Concrete
1948
Gift of the Artist
Beneath Lovejoy Ramp to the
Broadway Bridge

109
Unknown Artists
STAINED GLASS WINDOWS
Stained Glass
1873
Commission of Trinity Episcopal
Church
Trinity Episcopal Church
147 N.W. 19th

110
Anderson, C. Bryce
WINDOWS
Stained Glass
1927
Commission of Temple Beth
Israel
1931 N.W. Flanders

110
Gerlach, Albert A.
WINDOWS
Stained Glass
1927
Commission of Temple Beth
Israel
1931 N.W. Flanders

111
Hardy, Tom
WHOOPING CRANES
Sculpture—Bronze
1963
Commission of Physicians and
Surgeons Hospital
N.W. 19th and Lovejoy

112
Schiwetz, Jr., Berthold
ST. FRANCIS AND HIS
FRIENDS
Sculpture—Bronze
1966
Commission of Good Samaritan
Hospital and United States
Government
School of Nursing
1015 N.W. 22nd

113
Russo, Michele
UNTITLED
Sculpture—Steel
1955
Commission of Bill Fletcher
2745 N.W. Pettygrove

114
Izquierdo, Manuel
SILVER DAWN
Sculpture—Steel
1980
Commission of Metropolitan Arts
Commission, Portland
Development Commission,
Northwest District Association,
ESCO Corporation, and Harold
and Arlene Schnitzer
Wallace Park
N.W. 25th and Raleigh

115
Butler, Ken
UNTITLED (Clouds)
Mural—Acrylic on Cinderblock
1982
Commission of Portland
Development Commission
N.W. 26th and Thurman

116
Jellum, Keith
MIMIR
Sculpture—Bronze
1980
Commission of Portland
Development Commission and
Tom Walsh
N.W. 27th between Thurman
and Upshur

117
Littman, Frederic
THE FLOGGER
Sculpture—Steel
1968
Commission of ESCO
Corporation
N.W. 25th and Vaughn

118
Balazs, Harold
GARGOYLES
Sculptures—Copper
1979
Commission of Oregon School of
Arts and Crafts
8245 S.W. Barnes

118
Carpenter, Ed
UNTITLED
Stained Glass
1979
Commission of Oregon School of
Arts and Crafts
8245 S.W. Barnes

118
Jellum, Keith
UNTITLED
Sculpture—Bronze
1979
Commission of Oregon School of
Arts and Crafts
8245 N.W. Barnes

119
Cotter, David
POD 48
Sculpture—Fiberglass
1978
Commission of Oregon Art
Advocates and Oregon Arts
Commission
Catlin Gabel School
8825 S.W. Barnes

119
Goldsby, Al
TURTLES
Sculpture—Bronze
1968
Gift of Rosina and Howard
Morgan in Memory of Their Son,
Thomas
Catlin Gabel School
8825 S.W. Barnes

119
Hardy, Tom
DEER
Sculpture—Bronze
1975
Gift of Hans Frohman
Catlin Gabel School
8825 S.W. Barnes

119
Johnston, Lynn Oulman
UNTITLED
Sculpture—Aluminum
1964
Gift of Class of 1964
Catlin Gabel School
8825 S.W. Barnes

119
Johnston, Lynn Oulman
UNTITLED
Sculpture—Aluminum
1974
Gift of the Artist
Catlin Gabel School
8825 S.W. Barnes

119
Kelly, Lee
ELKHORN
Sculpture—Steel
1979
Gift of Friends in Memory of
Jason Kelly
Catlin Gabel School
8825 S.W. Barnes

119
Kelly, Lee
UNTITLED
Sculpture—Steel
1981
Gift of the Family of Helen
Elizabeth Wilson
Catlin Gabel School
8825 S.W. Barnes

120
Rose, "Buster"
LAST SUPPER
Relief—Wood
1979
Gift of the Artist
St. Vincent's Hospital
9205 S.W. Barnes

120
Setziol, LeRoy
UNTITLED
Relief—Teak
1971
Commission of St. Vincent's
Medical Foundation
St. Vincent's Hospital
9205 S.W. Barnes

121
Unknown Artist
STAINED GLASS WINDOW
Stained Glass
1889
Commission of St. John's
Episcopal Church of Milwaukie
Pioneer Church
S.E. Spokane and 6th

122
Kibby, Chuck
UROBOROS
Sculpture—Concrete
1980
Commission of U.S.
Comprehensive Employment and
Training Act
Westmoreland Park
S.E. McLoughlin and Bybee

123
Kelly, Lee and Bronson, Bonnie
(Assisted by Duniway School
Students)
UNTITLED
Sculpture—Steel
1975
Commission of Oregon Arts
Commission and National
Endowment for the Arts
7700 S.E. Reed College Place

124
Cunningham, Dennis
UNTITLED
Mural—Ceramic
1977
Commission of U.S.
Comprehensive Employment and
Training Act
Eastmoreland Golf Course
2425 S.E. Bybee

125
Littman, Frederic
UNTITLED (Young Girl Planting
Tree)
Relief Sculpture—Aluminum
1959
Commission of United States
National Bank of Oregon
4727 S.E. Woodstock

126
Kelly, Charles
UNTITLED
Sculpture—Steel
1974
Gift of Reed College Students and
Alumni in Memory of Professor
William Anderson
3203 S.E. Woodstock

126
Kelly, Lee
TRIGGER FOUR
Sculpture—Steel
1979
Gift of Mr. and Mrs. John Gray
Reed College
3203 S.E. Woodstock

126
Morris, Hilda
WINDGATE
Sculpture—Bronze
1980
Commission of Kaplan Fund
Linthicium Fund and Private
Donors
Reed College
3203 S.E. Woodstock

127
Berry, George
BENJAMIN FRANKLIN
Sculpture—Sandstone
1942
Commission of Alumni and
Students of Franklin High
School, the Portland School
Board and the Federal Arts
Projects (Subsidiary of the Works
Progress Administration)
5405 S.E. Woodward

128
Borglum, Gutzon
HARVEY W. SCOTT
Sculpture—Bronze
1933
Gift of the Scott Family
Mt. Tabor Park, S.E. 60th
between Yamhill and Division

129
Kriger, Colleen
UNTITLED
Window Shades—Linen
1978
Commission of U.S.
Comprehensive Employment and
Training Act
Multnomah County Public
Library, Belmont Branch
1038 S.E. 39th

130
Gerlach, Albert A.
WINDOWS
Stained Glass
1924
Commission of St. Stephen's
Catholic Church
1112 S.E. 41st

131
Franz, Evelyn
TRIAD
Sculpture—Steel
1979
Commission of Metropolitan Arts
Commission
Laurelhurst Park
S.E. 39th and Oak

132
West, Bruce
UNTITLED
Sculpture—Steel
1979
Commission of the Sisters of
Providence
Providence Hospital
4805 N.E. Glisan

133
Fremiet, Emanuel
JOAN OF ARC
Sculpture—Bronze
1924
Gift of Dr. Henry Waldo Coe
N.E. 39th and Glisan

134
Anderson, C. Bryce
WINDOWS
Stained Glass
1927
Commission of Holy Trinity
Greek Orthodox Church
3131 N.E. Glisan

135
Posner, Richard
THE CRYSTAL PALLETS:
DEFENCE OF LIGHT
Sculpture—Glass
1983
Commission of Multnomah
County One Percent for Public
Art
(Metropolitan Arts Commission)
Multnomah County Elections
Building
S.E. 11th and Morrison

136
Kelly, Lee
NASH
Sculpture—Steel
1979
Commission of National Builders
Hardware Company
1019 S.E. 10th

137
Clark, Geoffrey and Buckman
School Students
BUCKMAN NEIGHBORHOOD
MURAL
Mural—Acrylic on Cinderblock
1982
Commission of Buckman
Neighborhood and Buckman
School Students, Miller Paint
Company, Rodda Paint
Company, and National Builders
Hardware
S.E. 12th and Morrison

138
Moore, William and
Cunningham, Dennis
UNTITLED
Relief—Wood and Ceramic
1983
Commission of Oregon State One
Percent for Art (Oregon Arts
Commission)
Commission for the Blind
535 S.E. 12th

139
West, Bruce
UNTITLED
Fountain—Steel and Brick
1976
Commission of U.S.
Comprehensive Employment and
Training Act, the Collins
Foundation, the Oregon Arts
Commission and the Vest Pocket
Community Center
St. Francis Park, 1136 S.E. Oak

140
Stuhl, Jack (assisted by Ted
Widing and Phillips Electrical)
HOLLADAY PARK MUSICAL
FOUNTAIN
Fountain—Concrete, Music,
Lights
1964
Commission of Lloyd Corporation
and Pacific Power and Light
through Portland Rose Festival
Association
Holladay Park, N.E. 11th and
Multnomah

141
Heidel, Frederick
TREFOIL
Sculpture—Laminated Glass
1982
Commission of Lloyd Corporation
Lloyd Center Tower Building
825 N.E. Multnomah

141
Feves, Betty
CLEFT PATTERNS
Sculpture—Ceramic Relief
1982
Commission of Lloyd Corporation
Lloyd Center Tower Building
825 N.E. Multnomah

142
Fieldskov, Niels Valdemar
THE ICE SKATER
Sculpture—Wood
1855
Gift of Mrs. Justin Dees
Lloyd Center
N.E. 10th and Weidler

142
Hardy, Tom
FLIGHT OF BIRDS
Sculpture—Steel
1960
Purchase of Lloyd Corporation
Lloyd Center
N.E. 10th and Weidler

142
Izquierdo, Manuel
UNTITLED
Sculpture—Copper Relief
1958
Commission of Portland Federal
Savings Bank
Far West Federal Savings & Loan
1346 Lloyd Center

142
Jenson, Ray
HERONS AND WATER LILIES
Sculptures—Bronze
1960
Purchase by the Lloyd
Corporation
Lloyd Center
N.E. 10th and Weidler

142
Tsutakawa, George
UNTITLED
Sculpture and Fountain—Bronze
with Tile Base
1960
Commission of Lloyd Corporation
Lloyd Center
N.E. 10th and Weidler

143
Kelly, Lee (assisted by Pedr
Turner)
UNTITLED
Sculpture—Steel
1968
Commission of Portland
Development Commission
N. Failing and Kerby

144
Kaiser-Permanente Medical
Center
Changing Exhibits
Objects from the Center's Art
Collection
3414 N. Montana

145
Shamsud-Din, Isaac; Frison,
Henry; Harada, Jenny; Tatum,
Charles; Henderson, Chonitia;
Scott, Larry
ALBINA MURAL PROJECT
Murals
1978
Commission of U.S.
Comprehensive Employment and
Training Act
5200 N. Vancouver Avenue

146
Bitter, Carl
THOMAS JEFFERSON
Sculpture—Bronze
1915
Gift of Students of Jefferson High
School
5210 N. Kirby

146
Voisin, Adrian
LEWIS AND CLARK
MEMORIAL PLAQUE
Relief—Bronze
1935
Commission of Jefferson High
School Alumni Association and
the Works Projects
Administration
5210 N. Kerby

147
Allen, Jerry
DISC 4
Sculpture—Bronze
1978
Commission of U.S.
Comprehensive Employment and
Training Act
Peninsula Park, N. Albina and
Portland Blvd.

148
Coppini, Pompeii
GEORGE WASHINGTON
Sculpture—Bronze
1927
Gift of Dr. Henry Waldo Coe
N.E. 57th and Sandy

149
Kelly, Lee (Assisted by Bonnie
Bronson)
UNTITLED
Sculpture—Steel and Vitrified
Porcelain
1974
Commission of United States
National Bank of Oregon
7200 N.E. Fremont

150
Unknown Artists
Various Pieces
Reliefs and Sculptures—Marble,
Bronze, Wood
1924-1983
Commission of the Order of
Servants of Mary
The Grotto
N.E. 85th and Sandy

151
Miller, Michael
UNTITLED
Murals—Ceramic
1976
Commission of U.S.
Comprehensive Employment and
Training Act
4815 N.E. 70th

152
Bunce, Louis
UNTITLED
Painting—Acrylic on Canvas
1958
Commission of Port of Portland
Portland International Airport
N.E. Airport Way

153
Izquierdo, Manuel
THE FIGURE STRIDING
Sculpture—Steel
1962
Gift of University of Portland
Class of 1962
5000 N. Willamette

153
Kelly, Lee (Assisted by Bonnie
Bronson and John Kelly)
TREE OF LIFE
Sculpture—Steel, Nickel silver,
Enamel
1964
Commission of University of
Portland
5000 N. Willamette

153
Littman, Frederic
SEDES SAPIENTIAE
MADONNA AND CHILD
Relief Sculpture—Lead
1958
Commission of University of
Portland
5000 N. Willamette

153
Morandi, Tom
PAPA SIERRA
Sculpture—Steel
1980
Purchase by Students Cultural
Arts Board, Senior Class,
University of Portland and
Oregon Arts Commission
5000 N. Willamette

154
Littman, Marianne Gold
UNTITLED (Scenes of Fishing,
Agriculture, Industry)
Reliefs—Terra cotta
1954
Commission of United States
National Bank of Oregon
7340 North Philadelphia

155
Ballator, John, Assisted by
Bunce, Louis and La Mode, Eric
UNTITLED
Mural—Egg Tempera on Wall
1936
Commission of U.S. Treasury
Relief Arts Projects
St. Johns Post Office
8720 N. Ivanhoe

156
Hardy, Tom
GEESE IN FLIGHT
Sculpture—Bronze
1971
Gift of Elizabeth Ducey
Oregon Historical Society's
Bybee-Howell Territorial
Farmstead, Sauvie Island

157
Gillman, Steve
WIND PLANE
Sculpture—White Granite
1983
Commission of Multnomah
County One Percent for Public
Art (Metropolitan Arts
Commission)
Blue Lake Park, 205th and N.E.
Marine Drive, Troutdale

INDEX II
ARTISTS

Numbers refer to the numerical index (Index I) to Portland's Public Art Works, and to the corresponding locations on the maps contained in this guide.

MAPS

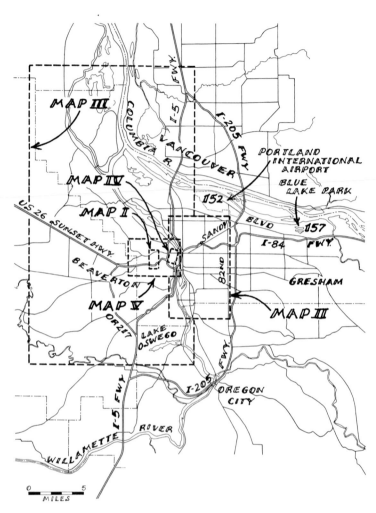

GREATER PORTLAND

BROKEN LINES INDICATE

MAP	WORKS
I	94-105
II	121-151
III	83-86, 118-120, 153-156
IV	1-77
V	78-82, 87-93, 106-117

GREATER PORTLAND: 152 & 157

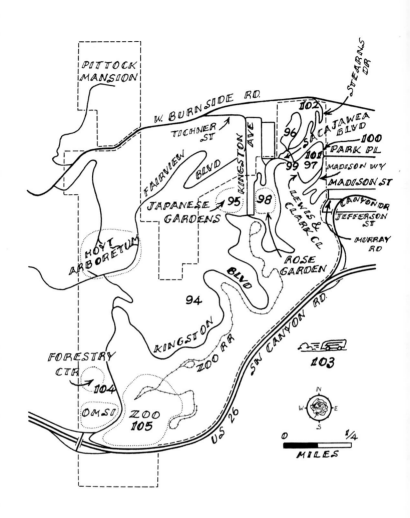

MAP I WASHINGTON PARK
WORKS 94-105

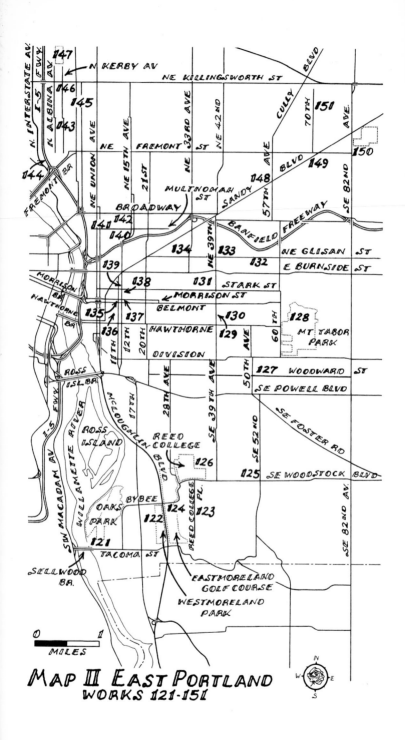

MAP III EAST PORTLAND
WORKS 121-151

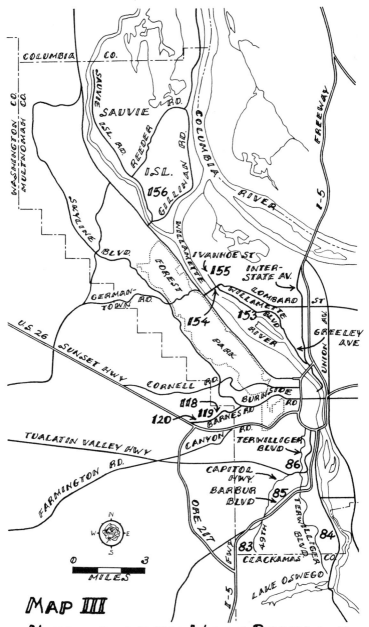

MAP III
METROPOLITAN WEST PORTLAND
WORKS 83-86, 118-120, 153-156

69

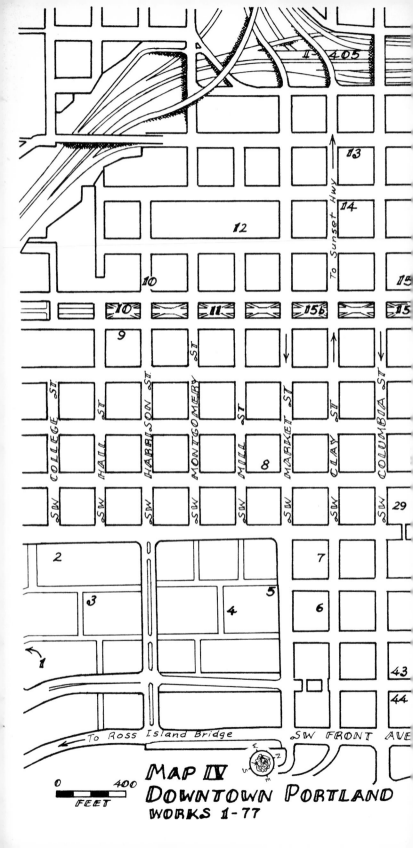

MAP IV
DOWNTOWN PORTLAND
WORKS 1-77

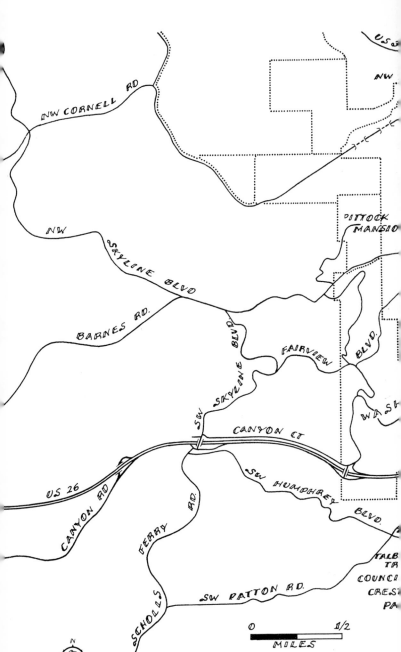

MAP V WEST PORTLAND
WORKS 78-82, 87-93, 106-117

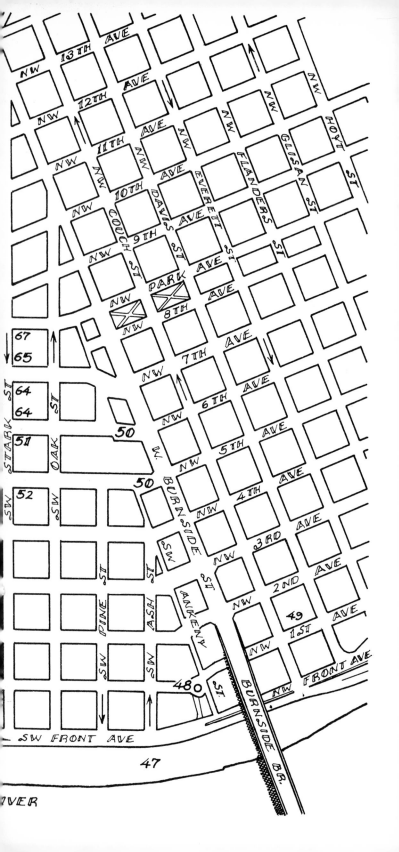

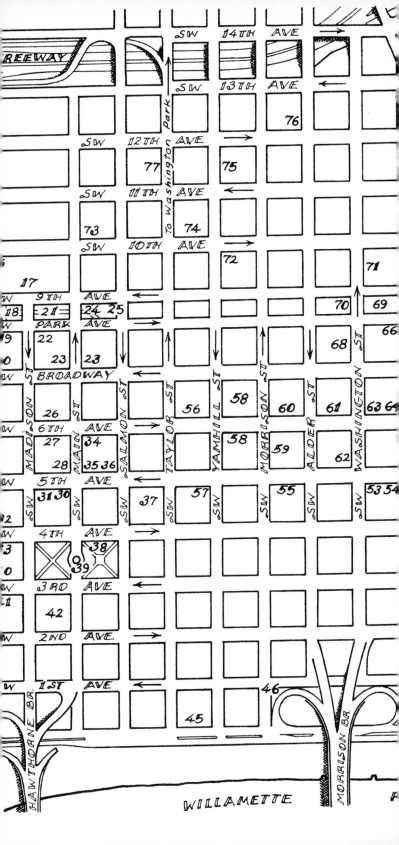